The Bin Men

Harold Henry Williams

Text copyright © Harold Henry Williams 2000
Illustrations, Heather Dickinson
Design, Andrassy Design 01 484 451700
Cover photograph, Stella Fitzpatrick
Editor, Stella Fitzpatrick
Published and distributed by Gatehouse Books Ltd.
Hulme Adult Education Centre, Stretford Road, Manchester M15 5FQ
First Printed in 2000, reprinted in 2005 by Oldham Colourprint Ltd 0161 633 2044
ISBN 0 906253 76 4
British Library cataloguing in publication data:
A catalogue record for this book is available from the British Library

The Bin Men was developed from writing originally produced by Harold Henry Williams
with his tutor Thelma Banks at Victoria Mill Adult Education Centre, Manchester.

Two Gatehouse Reading Circles recommended this story for publication. Many thanks for
their work to Nora Ashton, Irene Leech, Mary Morris and Josie Roche at Newton House &
Sandra Brown, Beverley Chadderton, Christine Jones, Gail Rocca, John Smith, Kevin
Summers and Hugh Walsh at Spurley Hey Centre.

Thanks also to basic skills groups run by Manchester Adult Education Services at the
Birtles, Greenheys, Newton House, Plant Hill and Varna Centres and to Moya Curran's
group in Stockport with whom we piloted a first draft of this book.

Gatehouse acknowledges grant aid towards the production of this book from The Peter
Kershaw Trust & Lloyds TSB Foundation for England & Wales, and ongoing financial
support from Manchester City Council and North West Arts Board.

Gatehouse is a member of The Federation of Worker Writers & Community Publishers.

Introduction

I was born at St. Mary's Hospital in Manchester, England on the 14th of October, 1946. It was just after the Second World War. I weighed in at ten pounds.

I went to Ashton Old Road School in Openshaw, also in Manchester. I was captain of the cricket team, but no good at reading and writing.

Then I went to an adult education centre, quite a few years later. That is where I met Thelma and Doreen. They were my tutors. They helped me a lot. My spelling, my reading and my writing have got better. I got some certificates. I got maths, English, computer, first aid and a few more skills. The certificates are framed, at home. All this was over five years.

I wrote this book, just to show you it can be done! It is all about me being a bin man for twenty five years. It was fun, being on the bins.

I like people. I will help anybody. Every year I played Father Christmas in the creche, at my centre. The first year my beard was pink! The last time it was a piece of cardboard with bits of cotton wool stuck on it. But the kids liked me a lot!

Enjoy the story,

Harold Henry Williams

At the back of the book, on page 22,
you'll find some of the words explained
in a glossary.

When I was a kid, there was a little guy
who was a dustbin man.
I used to watch him.
He would get three or four metal bins,
one inside the other,
and he would spin them round
with a finger, taking the empty bins
back down the entry.

He had this hook to open the yard doors
so he could put back the bins.
He carried it on his belt.

It just amazed me,
the way he spun them with his finger.
It made me want to be a dustbin man.

I worked as a dustbin man
for twenty five years.
I started when I was twenty, in 1966.
The lads I worked with got on well.
We became friends.

If they could help you out, they would.
If you lost your wages
they would have a whip round.
I am still in touch with them now,
over thirty years later.

When I worked on the bins,
there was a driver and two carriers.
Years before I started
there used to be a driver and four carriers.

One man would bring out the bins
to the front of the street,
two men would empty them,
and one would take them back.

One of the older men told me a story
about that time:
One day, they came to an entry
where there was an old lady
waiting for them. She was crying.

She said, "Would you do me a favour?
My dog has just died.
If I give you half a crown
could you take it away?"
The men said yes,
they would take the dog away.

The driver got a cloth across his arms
to carry the dog.
The other men walked behind,
doing the death march, to the dustcart.
Then he got some plastic flowers
and laid them around the dog.

The woman was still crying
when she went in the house.
The bin men went around the corner
to the other side of the entry.

The driver sent the back of the dustcart
up in the air. When it came down,
there was a big cloud of dust
and the dog jumped out.
It must have been in a coma.

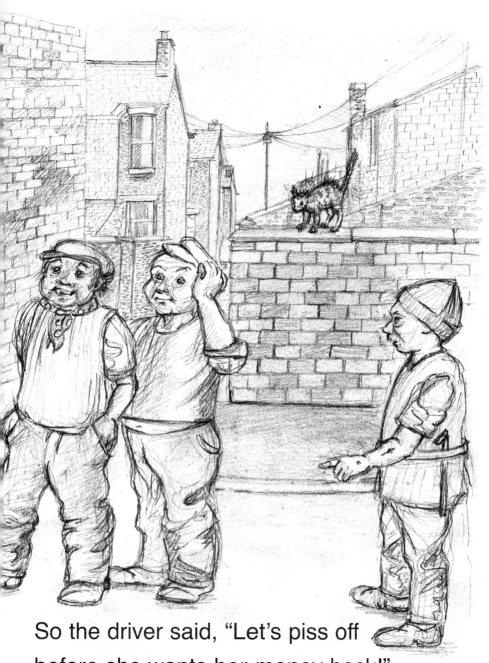

So the driver said, "Let's piss off before she wants her money back!"

A week later, the bin men went back
to empty the bins.
When they got there
the old lady was waiting for them
with a big smile on her face.

The dog was in the back yard
playing with its ball and running around.
"I don't know what you did
but it worked!" she said.
It was nice to see that woman
so happy with her dog.

The best day was Friday, wages day.
All the bin men were there
waiting for their wages, and larking about.
One Friday, three of us went in the yard
and saw two legs
sticking out of one of the wagons.
Have you ever seen artificial legs?
They look so real.
And these had trousers on, and shoes!

One of the carriers had stuck them
in the back of a wagon.
We thought someone was trapped.
We were panicking.
One of us pressed the safety button
on the back of the wagon
and the two legs fell out!
That is just two stories about the bin men.
I could tell you more!

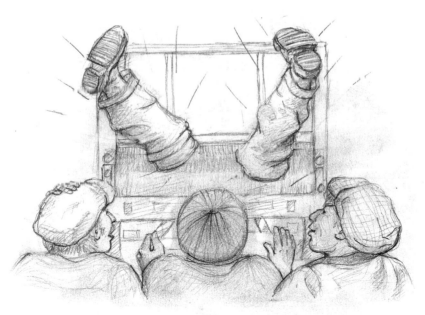

Glossary

This glossary explains the meaning of some words, as they are used in this book.

back yard (page 19)
a piece of hard ground at the back of your house

carriers (page 10)
the men who carry the dustbins to be emptied

death march (page 14)
a slow march, used at funeral processions

dustbin, bins (page 5)
a thing outside your house that you put rubbish in

dustbin man, bin man (page 5)
a man whose job is to take away your rubbish

dustcart (page 14)
a vehicle for collecting rubbish and taking it to the rubbish tip

entry (page 5)
a back alley between rows of old houses. See the picture on page 7

half a crown (page 13)
an English coin, no longer in use. Half a crown was a good tip (see opposite) back in 1960. But in today's English money it would be worth only 12½ pence

in a coma (page 16)

to be unconscious

lads (page 8)

the men who are your friendly workmates

larking about (page 20)

having fun

let's piss off (page 17)

we should go away quickly (regarded by some people as offensive)

safety button (page 21)

a switch to stop the machinery inside the dustcart

a tip (page 22)

a small extra amount of money which you give to someone who has done a job for you

wages (page 20)

the money you receive every week for the work you do

wagon (page 20)

a vehicle for collecting rubbish and taking it to the rubbish tip

whip round (page 9)

collecting money from a small group of people to give to someone else who deserves it

Gatehouse Books

Gatehouse is a unique publisher

Our writers are adults who are developing their basic reading and writing skills. Their ideas and experiences make fascinating material for any reader, but are particularly relevant for adults working on their reading and writing skills. The writing strikes a chord – a shared experience of struggling against many odds.

The format of our books is clear and uncluttered. The language is familiar and the text is often line-broken, so that each line ends at a natural pause.

Gatehouse books are both popular and respected within Adult Basic Education throughout the English speaking world. They are also a valuable resource within secondary schools, Social Services and within the Prison Education Service and Probation Services.

Booklist available

Gatehouse Books
Hulme Adult Education Centre
Stretford Road
Manchester
M15 5FQ
Tel: 0161 226 7152
Fax: 0161 868 0351
E-mail: office@gatehousebooks.org.uk
Website: www.gatehousebooks.org.uk

The Gatehouse Publishing Charity Ltd. is a registered charity, no. 1011042
Gatehouse Books Ltd. is a company limited by guarantee reg. no. 2619614